GOD, WHAT'S NEXT?

A Question,

A Leap of Faith!

Don Bunna

God, What's Next? A Question, A Leap of Faith!

ISBN: 979-8-9932461-0-9

"I can do all things through Christ who strengthens me."

Philippians 4:13 (NKJV)

To my daughter Amanda.
"Mouse"
The more you search, the quicker you will find peace and joy!

Table of Contents

1.
Telling Stories

"...Christ with me, Christ before me,
Christ behind me, Christ in me..."[1]

I love telling stories, especially the ones I am about to tell you. These are the remarkable moments in my life that have validated my Christian testimony. Some were filled with joy, others with pain, but all were very important in bringing me closer to the Lord. While traveling through my sojourns of faith, a few select words from St. Patrick's Breastplate Prayer best describes my faith journey and how the presence of Jesus Christ changed my life forever.

This journey has been, and still is, a long trek of good and difficult adventures. Some were sad, yet many became filled with fun and excitement. My stories talk about the reasons I lost my faith in God during my early adulthood, and stories that will talk about those empty years where my faith sat in the background of my life. There is also a fantastic story about my day of reckoning, coming in mid-life when I realized I needed Jesus more than life itself.

The main reason for losing my faith stemmed from the anger brought by trauma from a chaotic childhood. Blamed not only for my actions and behaviors but for the actions of others in the family, it gave way to anxiety and anger building up inside my youthful spirit. Raised Roman Catholic and attending Catholic school, with the teachings of Jesus loves me, gave me a challenge, arriving home from school to an unloving family and a home filled with much unrest and chaos. My young response was to make Jesus my immediate scapegoat, doing to him what others were doing to me.

Eventually, as a young adult, I would turn away from the Catholic Church and join a church within the Protestant Denomination, still, even then, my faith in Jesus was emotionally drained. As the years went on, I

---

[1] Irishcentral.com, St. Patrick's Breastplate: the prayer of Ireland's patron saint.

would attend Worship service, but as a non-committal bystander, until the day everything in my life changed!

It was on a road trip traversing the curves in the Smoky Mountain Range on a summer afternoon in June of 2006, that my life changed. Oh, how it changed! I was going to visit my daughter living near Savanah, GA. Due to certain events taking place before my departure, I had become dramatically despondent, totally consumed to the point I wanted to end my life. Something spiritual inside of me, I know not to this day, caused me to cry out to Jesus for forgiveness because I couldn't go on by myself any longer. Suddenly, I heard a spiritual voice and felt a windy presence engulf me. A presence like I had never felt came upon me, creating a life-changing moment within.

And so began a faith journey that has spanned almost 2 decades and continues to this day. A faith journey that has taught me more lessons on how to live my life than I ever dreamed possible. It has been a pilgrimage that has shown me the pathway to my redemption and salvation, and it is and always will be through the Cross and the grace of Jesus Christ given to me through his love! I've learned that I can't earn Christ's grace; it's given to me freely, just because!

There were many aspects of my rediscovered Christian faith that I would begin to explore upon returning home from that road trip. My circumstances had not changed, but how I viewed my condition did! The deeper you place yourself inside your faith in Christ, the greater your spiritual and emotional stamina becomes when faced with the perils of the perfect storms of life.

Within 1 ½ years, upon returning from my road trip, I would begin dating a new girlfriend who would become my wife. We shared so much of life, most importantly, our faith in Jesus Christ. We also shared the love of riding motorcycles together. But just as wonderful things come into one's life, unfortunate developments often follow. A devastating motorcycle accident would soon whisk away my bride, leaving my soul void of peace and joy.

Several weeks later, my dear friend and long-time pastor would guide me through this loss, delicately telling me, there are no answers to all the "*why*" questions, but now it is time to begin asking God, what comes next. So, as I asked God what was to come next in my life, I soon realized a couple of obstacles that would grow into a crucible of enormous weight had been placed at my proverbial front doorstep.

Today, the crucible is off my shoulders! It took many years of long travels, teaching moments, lessons learned, unearthing, and letting go of childhood and youthful traumas to realize I was carrying guilt for many things that were not my fault. It was finally time to let it all go, to forgive others and myself! It also took learning that true peace and joy come from the grace given to us by our Lord and Savior Jesus Christ and are not reliant on another human being.

The day I traveled high up in the Smokies was the most fantastic day of my life, as it was the day I chose to turn toward the Cross and Jesus and not away. Becoming much closer to my faith and having read more of my Bible in the last few years than I have in my entire life, I have developed a liking for the apostle Paul. Thinking about the life of Paul and as a Pharisee to the early Christians, he was not a good man. He was a bad man turned good man. So, if I looked in my rearview at the man I used to be, I would see a man I was not proud of, a man of whom I was ashamed.

I am looking forward to seeing the man Jesus is molding me to be. To say one thing about the day of my road trip in the Smoky Mountains, it was my Road to Damascus.

This is a story of my faith journey, the wonders of the Cross, and the grace of Jesus Christ. It is my story of how he blessed me as I traveled along my Road to Damascus. It was also during the most tragic time in my life and the many subsequent years, through God's grace, I was able to take A Leap of Faith. With that leap, I heard a Voice, I harnessed a Fresh Wind, allowing me a way to walk through those barren places which the obstacles and crucible created, and come out on the Other Side of Life with a sacred flow living my life for Jesus Christ.

Arriving at my Other Side of Life is my metaphor for feeling that whatever happens today, whether it is a good day or a day I am having a few struggles, my firm and undeniable faith in Christ will carry me through. It's a feeling of peace and joy, a feeling I had yearned for, for a long time. It is not a feeling of perfection but knowing I belong to a family overseen by the most perfect being imaginable, Jesus Christ!

This is my story of how I rebuilt my life, living for Christ and learning a few essential lessons. The first is knowing how to love myself and learning self-forgiveness; the second is learning true peace and joy, which comes to us through the Cross and the grace of Jesus Christ. And third, I will still have struggles in life! But since I've arrived at my Other Side of Life, I live with peace and joy in my heart and soul these days, and because I live my life for Christ, even with my struggles, my future will still be good!

So, let's get started!

2.
Me, the Road, Setting the Crucible

"When You Learn How to Die,
You Learn how to Live."[2]
-Morrie Schwartz

Sitting comfortably in my saddle, I watched the road pass by at 75mph. With nothing but a few pieces of safety gear, the experience left a lasting impact on me. Riding a motorcycle is undoubtedly not for everyone, but riding changed my attitude toward living and dying.

I knew exactly what I wanted to achieve when I started my first cross-country ride in the summer of 2011. It was the completion ride that would finish the 2010 Smoky Mountain Trip, which took the life of my wife, Kathy! I was aware of all the particulars of the ride, but as time went on, my faith and spirit would come face to face with more than my loss of Kathy.

First, before the ride started, some serious business needed to be taken care of. Just a few months before, officially inside a courtroom, I had forgiven the person who had recklessly driven into Kathy and me at a speed of 60mph, killing her and sending me into an NDE/SDE! After many months of contemplation and prayer, I recommended no jail time for the person guilty of stupidity and carelessness, which is all he was guilty of! And after the court hearing, I sat with him, hugged him, and forgave him.

To better understand, I need to go back a few short steps to explain how a couple of obstacles and that central crucible came about.

During the evening of July 9, 2010, shortly after leaving home for what was to be a 9-day vacation in the Smoky Mountains, my wife, Kathy, and I were involved in a motorcycle accident. Caught in an unexpected rainstorm, we pulled to the shoulder of the road. After dismounting, we stood beside our motorcycles to wait out the storm. But then a tragic and heartbreaking freak accident took place, striking deep into the depths of

---

[2] Schwartz, Morrie. Tuesdays with Morrie. Kindle, Page 121

my spiritual core. My wife Kathy and I, newlyweds, were hit head-on by an out-of-control car that veered onto the shoulder of the roadway, forcing Kathy and me on a journey to heaven.

But as we were traveling through a wormhole, holding hands, a great force would be pulling on Kathy's other hand. Suddenly, I would lose hold of her, she would continue her travels to heaven, but my ride would be cut short. I would then hear a voice calling to me, "Come back," which was a young man caring for me at the accident scene. Later, in discussing my experience in detail to an expert in the field of Near-Death Experiences, Dr. Jeffrey Long, MD, would document my event as a Near-Death Experience and a Shared Death Experience.[3]

Several weeks after the accident of July 9, 2010, I found myself sitting with my dear friend, who was also my long-time pastor, asking him a troubling question: "Why did this happen? We were both hit by the car at the same time! Why didn't I die too?" He responded in a caring voice, paraphrasing, "My dearest friend, the questions you ask will never have answers. The question you may want to ask now is, 'God, what's next!'"

I needed to ask God what would come next in my life, and I knew that would pose a problem. Only a few had known of my severely blemished past, from youth into adulthood, and one of those few was Kathy. I had worked the better part of my life keeping my past hidden from the outside world, all the emotional scars I was severely ashamed of, all the years I had let my anger get the best of me, and I kept that hidden from my pastor.

But as I pondered the question he had presented me and all the issues that came to mind, I knew one thing: God knew every blemish that had ever crossed my path. I had been running away from my past for so long that I didn't know how to ask God what was to come next. I knew I must face all the emotional demons that had been preying on my mind for most of my life. So, now it's time to ask!

God, what's next for my life?

---

[3] Dr. Jeffrey Long, MD. Near Death Experience Research Foundation, Rolling Meadows, IL. Nderf.org, Don B NDE 16050 Submission date 11/4/2010

God, how do I find redemption and salvation for my past?

God, I was supposed to protect Kathy, and I didn't!

God, how do I find redemption and salvation for letting Kathy die?

God, what's next for my life?

The crucible had been set!

Did I think a cross-country motorcycle trip would solve all my problems?

No, but it seemed like the right way at the time!

I would soon realize that buried inside this crucible was another obstacle that would take me on an even deeper faith journey than I had ever imagined.

You see, regardless of all the teachings I went through attending a Catholic Elementary School for 8 years, with such a very chaotic home life, it never really stuck in my mind that my forever peace and joy came from my Savior Jesus Christ. So, as a result, I spent most of my adult life searching for peace and joy through human contact, which I never received until Kathy came into my life. When Kathy died, so did my peace and joy. Thus came the added obstacle buried within the crucible.

How do I deal with this obstacle?

How do I crush this crucible?

Those were the questions confronting me at the same time I was asking the question,

God, what's next for my life?

This was all happening shortly after I had just lost my wife in a motorcycle accident!

So why a motorcycle road trip?

Riding on the open road gave me serenity, a unique perspective, a feeling of purity, and a cleanliness of nature. I could reach out for clarity about my future while on two wheels, knowing there was nothing but road rash and death underneath me. On the road, I had many deep conversations with Jesus. Have you ever had a particular place you would go to have those intimate talks with Jesus? The talks you have when you feel out of sorts or confused, and have doubts about your faith!

Jesus and I had many conversations during a total of 7 cross-country trips over 6 years, and the strength of my inner self grew stronger as did my faith. With each ride, we talked about how I needed to fit redemption into my life, how I needed to look at salvation from a different point of view, and how I should focus primarily on forgiveness for myself. According to Jesus, I was learning to forgive the many people who had wronged me but still found it hard to forgive myself for the wrongs I had done to others. Hmm, he could have a point!

Along the way, on each ride, Jesus and I also talked a lot about peace and joy and how we receive peace and joy through his grace. There were many talks about letting go of the past. I couldn't change the past and had no idea what the future holds, it was about time I began to live in the present, giving life my best shot, now! With each trip and with many other life situations that would be taking place in the coming years, the walls surrounding what I felt was an insurmountable crucible would begin to crumble!

With each long trip and with each mile traveled, I continued to grab a fresh wind while bridging the many crossroads I met. And with each "What's Next" question I asked of God, I came home with a feeling of hope that as the days passed, I would take the lessons I had learned from the road and use them to nurture my faith and become more aligned with God's will. It would be on the 2011 Florida trip I would experience a special kind of grace moment that would again bring changes to my life.

I'll write more about that grace moment and my other rides later, but let's move on to my early years. This will better explain how a Catholic school Altar boy could lose faith.

3.
Where the Journey Begins

"You have power over your mind – not outside events.
Realize this, and you will find strength."
– Marcus Aurelius[4]

So, here is where it all begins. I'll make it brief, the best I can, but without a quick flashback, it's a bit hard to understand how a young Altar boy, going to 8 years of Catholic School, growing up in the '60s, could drift as far from his faith as I did.

My life began in a chaotic, dysfunctional way. I was born in Chicago to divorcing parents and raised by grandparents, living with aunts and uncles who were barely older than me. As a grandchild, my grandparents spoiled me, soon making me the outcast with my aunts and uncles! This, in turn, would cause them to blame me for much of the wrong taking place in their lives, which began my initial anxieties. I developed a relationship with my mother and sister, but never with my biological father. I would often wonder what I did wrong as an infant for my biological father to disown me as he did. That wondering haunted me for many years, into adulthood.

Those eight years of Catholic Elementary school brought their own set of anxieties to my life. Many days, I was bullied by the big kids, as I had a growth disorder and was much smaller than all the other kids. And then getting similar treatment from the nuns made it easy for me to look forward to arriving home and hiding in my bedroom. From childhood through teen years, a battle would rage between my mother and grandparents, they claiming they saved me from adoption, my mother claiming they kidnapped me from her.

As stepfamilies were involved, my grandma was my step-grandma, which created more family squabbles. My stepfamily believed all the problems between the two families would be over if I were to be given back to my mother or an adoption agency. The problem was that it was the

---

[4] Aurelius, Marcus. Meditations. Translated by George Long, Book 4, Section 3, Dover Publications, 1997.

adoption agency my grandparents saved me from in the first place, or so they would tell me!

There it is, a very chaotic family tree, and the early development of my anxieties and anger issues. I spared you all the grim details as they have no place here in these writings; suffice to say, the details were harsh and made me wonder many times, where was God?

Teen years went by quickly, and not being much of an athlete, my attention turned to fast cars! By that time in my life, lacking any faith-based discipline within my home, I had drifted far away from my faith in Jesus. For me, Sunday mornings were for the drag strip and not church. For as much as I was raised in a Catholic environment, taught about the fatherly love of God, by the time I had reached my teens, I had always been surrounded by earthly father figures who either walked away, ignored, disowned, or showed love by the slap of a leather belt! I would leave the Catholic Church in my late teens, joining a church within the Protestant denomination. Still, by then, I was already running on empty as far as any organized religion was concerned.

So, there you have it! A flashback of my childhood to youth and my spiritual struggles growing up. There were many days I would ask Jesus to take me away, find me a new family, or just let me die. Well, Jesus wasn't going to take me away, he wasn't going to have a delivery truck drop off a new family, and he certainly wasn't going to let me die! Jesus would let me live my life, making the silly mistakes I made, while he patiently waited for me to take my road trip in the Smoky Mountains and learn the many lessons of life and faith I have been learning.

I'm now many years past the issues of my childhood, and my crucible has been crushed. I've grown much older than my grandparents were when they began raising me. Through my faith in Jesus, which has carried me through much these days, I've developed a unique way to review my past with a more positive outlook. Looking in the rearview mirror and seeing the enormous responsibilities my grandparents took on back then, I am simply amazed! They were newlyweds in their mid-40s during the 1950s, taking on the responsibility of stepfamilies, buying a new home in a newly incorporated town 40 miles south of Chicago in what was then the middle of nowhere, soon to be known as an extraordinary place for returning GIs from WWII to settle. They then started a new business and threw into the mix, raising a newborn grandson! Wow! I would say, Amazing, Daring, and Compassionate! That is all I can say! Did they have their shortcomings? Yes! Many, but we all have many shortcomings. Jesus did not choose people without shortcomings. He chose people who were imperfect and flawed, like my grandparents,

As my years went on, I learned more about their lives before they married each other. Both lived through tough times. Both had parents who showed little love. They were both young adults with young families at the start of the Great Depression. My grandpa came from a strict Catholic home environment, while my grandma came from a strict Baptist home and converted to Catholicism when she married my grandpa. Both had lost their earlier spouses to death.

Re-examining life through separate lenses has allowed me to see my childhood uniquely. It certainly did not take away the emotional damage done to my life. However, it did shine a different light on the many causal reasons for their behaviors and actions. That gave me a better feeling to say they did the best they could, given the tools they had in their personal toolboxes at those times in their lives.

Life is not easy, parenting is not easy, and I have come to understand that living life through my Christian faith is not easy. All of it takes challenging work, daily intentionality, and many times making decisions that are not easy to make. But, with prayers and the guidance of Jesus, those choices make us good. Neither were good at parenting nor showing love, but with only an 8th-grade education, both became successful business owners in a start-up town. Granted, my home life was chaotic; it wasn't faith-based, but in their own way, my grandparents were faithful people. A bit later in my writings, I will tell you how an old Bible my grandma gave me was pivotal in directing my spiritual life.

During my senior year in high school, I met a cute girl who took my breath away! We began to date, fell in love, and were married after we both graduated from high school. Soon, our son would be born, and as both of us aspired for college, the stress of a teen marriage and raising a child began to take its toll on our young marriage. The pressure became too much for us to manage. Our marriage would soon erode, and we would be divorced.

I had now grown into young adulthood, working in sales, and had recognized that the anger and anxieties were playing havoc with me. Still, my life had become preoccupied with activities that were not close to being faith-based, partying! I was divorced, had become estranged from my son, and at night, I was partying. But my anxieties and anger still lingered after the partying! The longer I stayed away from my faith and Christ, the deeper my anger bore its infectious disease into the depths of my heart and soul. I did seek therapy, but not being faith-based, it was ½ hour of talking and a prescription for an antidepressant. It was the 1970s, and an era in which talking about your personal feelings was uncommon.

Then, one winter morning in 1979, I met a bubbly hostess at a breakfast café and asked her for a date. She said yes, and that's how 26 years of good times, not so good times, began. We were very much opposites, but we had magnetic chemistry between us. We married, I finished college, and soon our daughter was born. We loved each other dearly, but after many years, the part about being opposites wore thin. We began arguing about trivial things that were not good for us or our daughter. We divorced, but soon reconciled and remarried.

After moving cross-country for my job, Chicago to OKC, and after those many years, 26 total, the difficulties finally took their toll, and it all came tumbling down. The differences of being opposites brought different expectations for us, and as those expectations became unfulfilled, tensions grew on both sides. We were blessed to bring into this world a beautiful daughter, now a grown woman and a wonderful mom herself. In the end, realizing our relationship had become "a square peg in a round hole" solidified our need for a 2nd and final divorce.

We attended church often during our time together, primarily to provide a faith foundation for our daughter. For me, attending church was still a Sunday morning ritual for an hour or two. Attend Worship service, drink coffee, shake a few hands, and get home in time for Sunday football or basketball! It was something I needed to do, like mow the lawn. By that time in my life, I was spiritually spent, drained, holding an invisible sign that said, "Hey Church, I'm Out of Order!"

It was February 2005, a time of significant confusion for me. As much as it was a mutual decision, my long-time marriage ended. My relationship spanned 26 years of my life, and suddenly, my life had been turned upside-down, shaken up, and dramatically changed. I found myself struggling for spiritual nourishment. I was ashamed of the person I had become. I had let the troubles of my past, the anxieties, the anger issues, and the pains from my childhood and youth consume me for so many years. I had lost two marriages, and my teenage daughter seemed to have lost her faith and her way in life. I was a broken and shattered man, feeling lost and needing to find a new way.

Searching for redemption for all I had done wrong, I knew there was only one way I could be saved, through the Cross and Jesus Christ. Now living alone and feeling quite lonely, I began rummaging through some old boxes one evening. I came across the Bible that my grandma had given me before she died many years prior. Flipping through the pages, I came upon a verse that put it all together for me, "For I know the plans I have for you," declares the Lord, "plans to prosper you and not harm you, plans to give you hope and a future." (Jeremiah 29:11 NIV). Hope, Future? I began to cry! How do I find hope and a new future?

No doubt about it! I must find my way back to my faith in Christ, or I would surely drown in the ocean of guilt and despair surrounding me. I could sense my faith in Christ was still floating deep down inside my soul, but I felt I had lost, most importantly, my hope, and wasn't sure how to get it back! Since I was not fond of organized religion, I wondered if I should give the church another chance. I had heard of a progressive United Methodist Church in the area where I lived, and I chose to "think" about attending!

4.
My Road to Damascus

"Map out your future – but do it in pencil. The road ahead is as long as you make it. Make it worth the trip."
— Bon Jovi[5]

"In their hearts humans plan their course, but the Lord establishes their steps." -Proverbs 16:9 (NIV). As I was "thinking" about attending that Methodist church, I soon found myself sitting in a pew at a Sunday Worship service at that church. Returning to Worship would not be the only way to bring me back to Christ, but it was a start. As I continued to attend Sunday Worship service, I knew more was needed, as on many days, the demons of despair were winning the battle for my soul. Feelings of failure abound inside of me, and with much time on my hands, as I had been downsized from a senior management position, I decided to take a road trip to visit my children. After visiting my son, still living in Chicago, I turned the car toward the southeast via the Great Smoky Mountains Range to see my daughter. Little did I know what Jesus had waiting for me during that road trip!

Driving along the highway, I couldn't shake a feeling of emptiness. I was not reconnecting with my faith as quickly as I had hoped. I attended Worship service every Sunday, yet I still felt distant from Jesus. The void would fade on Sunday mornings but would gain ground soon afterward, dragging me back into an abyss of guilt and shame. Little did I know, behind the scenes, Jesus was preparing me for the best of times, the worst of times, and many grace moments to come in my life. It was a time when I would become quite familiar with the apostle Paul and several of his letters.

So, there I was, driving through the Great Smoky Mountains, north of Asheville, NC. Setting the stage, it is now June 2006. I was divorced from a long-time marriage for 1 year, downsized from a senior management accounting position, had no job prospects on the horizon, felt out of sorts and depressed, and my relationship with Jesus remained distant. Was it me? Was I not trying hard enough? Was it Jesus? Was

---

[5] Bon Jovi. "Livin on a Prayer." Slippery When Wet, Mercury Records, 1986

Jesus tired of my false starts? Was Jesus saying to me, "Sorry, Don, three strikes and you're out!" I began to think this could be the time to end it all. Just drive the car right over the edge of the mountain. But something kept me from doing it, and as tears welled in my eyes, I grabbed a CD from the pile next to me and put it in the player, and a song began to play. It was Jesus Take the Wheel[6] and as the song played, I cried out for Jesus to help me because I couldn't go on any longer by myself. Suddenly a Presence washed over me like I had never felt before, and I heard a spiritual voice telling me, "All will be okay. Jesus is with you and always has been. He has never left your side. Trust in the Lord." It was then that I felt the Holy Spirit re-light the pilot light inside my soul.

That day, I was granted a gift from Jesus Christ, a grace moment that would begin the changes about to come in my life. On that day, hugging the curving roads through the Smokies, I discovered Christ doesn't count strikes! Balls or strikes, he wants us to keep running the bases because every time we swing the bat, we hit a home run for Christ. And He doesn't much care about how many false starts we have because with Jesus, every start is a start for Him. The Psalmist David wrote, "…though he may stumble, he will not fall, for the Lord upholds him with his hand." (Psalm 37:24 NIV).

During that drive through the Smokies, a time when I felt nothing but despair, listening to a Christian song, and hearing spiritual voices I came to the realization, as much as I had chosen a specific direction for my life many years before, by the glory of God's free will given to me, I could change my path to be more positive and travel a different yet exciting new way. On that day, I was given an opportunity to rediscover my faith, and I chose the Cross and Jesus Christ.

It became a road trip that changed the entire landscape of my life, which will forever be known as my Road to Damascus. We read in Acts 9:18, ESV, *"And immediately something like scales fell from his eyes, and he regained his sight."* I didn't have scales covering my eyes, but I was blind to the truth of my need for Jesus being in my life. During that drive in the Smokies, my invisible scales fell off, allowing my sight to be restored so that I could see the truth.

---

[6] Carrie Underwood. "Jesus Take the Wheel." Some Hearts, Arista Nashville, November 15, 2005, Track # 4, Compact Disc

5.
Coulda, Shoulda, Woulda

"The one who gets wisdom loves life;
the one who cherishes understanding will soon prosper."
— Proverbs 19:8 (NIV)

Once I chose the Cross and Jesus, my life was set on a new trajectory, much different from what I had planned. That choice didn't create a perfect or magical life for me; however, it did push me to develop a different outlook on life, with a more peripheral view. Improved opportunities came my way, and I began to look at life with a positive feeling. And yes, I would soon meet a blue-eyed Irish country girl, fall in love, marry, and we would enjoy many happy days together.

But unfortunately, grief would soon overtake the peace and joy I had come to find in my love for Kathy. Grappling with Kathy's death and my loss of peace and joy, questions about my faith would soon bubble to the surface, forcing me to look at the foundation my Christian faith was built on. I wondered how one discovers forever peace and joy! I had finally found peace and joy with Kathy, but when she died, so did my peace and joy! Why!

Waking up the morning of Saturday, July 10, 2010, and coming to grips with the events of the previous evening brought much uncertainty to my life. As each day came along, I hoped to stay strong within my faith to provide the stamina needed to deal with the emotional hurts and pains of my past, the driving force behind my feelings of self-blame.

Dealing with the psychological questions, such as why I am still here or was Kathy's death my fault, would become my emotional traveling companion for many years. At times, I would find myself falling into a deep, shadowy world known as the *Dark Night of the Soul,* a dark zone a certain few travel along during their spiritual journey. But it can also be a place of spiritual awakening, discovery, and evolution, where valuable lessons can be learned. I would find myself drifting in and out of that world, at varied times throughout the next 10 years of my life, learning many important lessons with one standout: no words, actions, thoughts, or wishes can ever change the past!

Three words would cast a spell over me and take me to the shadowy world! Coulda, Shoulda, Woulda. Those words haunted me for years. Could life have been different if we had left on another day? Should we have chosen another destination? Would things have turned out differently? Maybe. But I've learned that living in the land of 'what ifs' only keeps you trapped in guilt. No matter how much I replay that night, nothing can change it. What I can change is how I live today. The lesson I've taken from those haunting questions is this: regret has no power to rewrite the past, but faith can redeem the present

So, as time went on, so did lessons of life being taught to me, and a few more events would alter the course I had been traveling on. Realizing that my life would never be the same did not come easily. Kathy was my wife, friend, lover, and Anam Cara, which in Gaelic means *"Soul Friend."* She was The One I had been searching for an exceptionally long time. Given my mental state, regrets can easily resurface and upset me, so I needed to remain vigilant.

As 3 months had passed since the day of the accident, my bonus daughter Beth began to plan family time away for the following June, feeling it would provide much-needed spiritual healing. The plan was to vacation along Florida's Gulf coast with members of Kathy's Florida family. But first, we had a significant emotional hurdle to deal with. The court hearing for the driver of the car that killed Kathy was just around the corner.

The hearing finally occurred nine months after the accident, in April 2011. The charges were Negligent Homicide-Motor Vehicle. During that entire time, I prayed for Jesus to give me the wisdom and the discernment to make the right recommendation to the District Attorney. I also considered the circumstances and the facts, now nine months later. He had been driving carelessly, anxious to get home, and was not under the influence of drugs or alcohol. Should I recommend to the DA that he go to jail for something I may have done at some time in my life?

With much consideration, many prayers, and in agreement with my family, I recommended no jail time. After the judge informed him of the recommendation and her agreement, I met him for the first time after the court hearing. I knew I was meeting a man who was filled with remorse and spiritually broken. As I hugged him, I told him he had been forgiven by so many, and it was now time for him to go home and learn how to forgive himself.

That is what I told him: learn to forgive yourself! Wow, precisely one of the main ingredients in my quest in learning how to find peace and joy again in life! The apostle Paul reminds us, *"Bear with each other and forgive one another if any of you has a grievance against someone. Forgive as the Lord forgave you."* (Colossians 3:13 NIV). I found it to be a bit ironic, as I listened to the Holy Spirit, living inside of me, using wisdom and courage to make the right decision for this man's future. Yet, it would take a few more years and several more miles for me to cross, before I would understand that same lesson about forgiving myself.

As I look back today, that day in court was another point of preparation Jesus was doing with me. I know for sure there was more than just the driver who received a gift from God that day! A gift was given to me wrapped with a bow, but it took me a few more years to unwrap it. How many times do we look past what is right before our eyes?

And so, the summer arrived, and choices were made. I chose to go on that trip, and I chose to ride my motorcycle. Was I ready for a long cross-country trip, both physically and emotionally? The ride would be over 3,000 miles, round-trip. I needed that time away, near the ocean, clearing my mind and refreshing my spirit. My plans were beach time with the family, ride to the Smokies to complete Kathy's and my ride, ride the Tail of the Dragon, and head home.

Little did I know that the day I left my garage to begin the long ride to Florida would be the first day of a long Odyssey that would last 6 years and involve seven cross-country solo motorcycle trips encompassing over 24,000 cross-country miles. It would also be the catalyst for many major life-altering decisions, create many new memories, and provide spiritual lessons that would, again, change the trajectory of my life.

So, God, What's Next?

6.
Some Things Just Can't Be Explained, Rider of the Storm

"And in all your comings and goings, may you ever have a kindly greeting from them you meet along the road."

As I continued to ask God what was next in my life, I would follow what I felt were His directives. At times, I would float in and out of the dark side, trying ever so hard to stay close to my faith in Christ, knowing if I did, I would find my way to a clear path. I had survived the big hurdle of the court hearing; afterward, it was beach time. Time for gearing down, visiting Kathy's Florida family, and enjoying the sand and surf. It was a planned 4 days of travel to Florida on two wheels before meeting with my bonus kids.

The first 2 days were relatively uneventful, but the 3rd day of travel brought about an incident I can only describe as a divine intervention and a grace moment. About 50 miles west of Tallahassee, the winds began to howl, and the sky filled with dark, ominous clouds. Knowing I needed to find my way to the shoulder of the road to dismount and put on my rain gear was giving me the jitters. I knew this trip would be long, and I would eventually have to ride through rain, but I hoped it would not be on the third day of travel.

This would be the first time riding in the rain since the accident of July 9, 2010, and I knew I had to stay calm, or fear and anxiousness would begin to take over my body. Light rain pellets started to drop, and I began to tremble, holding my handlebars tightly. Scanning the roadway, all I could see were cars and trucks, no motorcycles! Seeing a viaduct ahead, I made my way to its shoulder, turned off my motorcycle, dismounted, and as I did, suddenly, out of nowhere came another motorcycle rider who pulled over in front of me, also to put on his rain gear. I was certain no motorcycles were around me. Who was he and where did he come from; this rider from nowhere, like an angel appearing out from the storm.

His calm presence was like a shield, and somehow, he knew just what to say. We talked about where we lived, and the reasons for our travels. I told him of the accident 11 months prior. He had this "special way" about him, as if he already knew of the accident and knew it was the first rainstorm I had ridden in since the accident. With deepness to his voice, tears rolling down his cheeks, he told me how sorry he was for my loss. The words we spoke to each other were uncanny. I had this spiritual feeling inside that he had been divinely directed there to aid me. This man, this rider of the storm, whom I had never met, seemed to know all about me, and was giving me this calming effect.

Fifteen minutes had passed, and as we zipped up our rain gear, we shook hands and said goodbye. He said he was happy he stopped, saying, paraphrased, "when I first pulled over and dismounted, I could see a look of fear on your face." That comment puzzled me. He was confident that his presence and our talking helped remove my fear. I graciously thanked him, and as we mounted our bikes, seeing a clear break in traffic, we rode away from the shoulder within seconds of each other. The rain had turned to a light drizzle, and as I looked around, up and down the roadway, I could not see him. He was gone!

This rider, whom I had just spent 15 minutes with, had disappeared! I stretched my eyesight as far as possible, but he was nowhere to be seen! Strange! The light drizzle continued for several hours, and I arrived in Tallahassee with a sense of calmness and much wonder! As I said my nightly prayers that evening, I gave special thanks to Jesus for sending me what I felt to be my biker guardian angel to show me the way when I felt my way was in doubt.

The time spent with family was enjoyable. Many laughs, tears, and stories about Kathy and the crazy things she and her cousin Ann did in their younger years. Finally, my last night had come, and I would say good night as I would begin my ride to the Smoky Mountains the next morning. A 3-day trip, and as I leaned back in my saddle, coming out of a huge curve, the Smoky Mountain Range was staring at me. Raising my hand as if to say to Kathy, we made it, a yellow and purple butterfly quickly came to rest on my hand and flew away. Kathy's two favorite colors! A message from heaven? Yes, I do believe so!

As I parked my motorcycle and checked into the hotel, I pondered, *now what?* I realized I did not have the emotional or spiritual stability to ride the Tail of the Dragon, 318 Curves in 11miles! It had not been a year since Kathy's funeral, and I decided the Dragon would have to wait another time: my 2013 Road Trip. As the evening wore on, I walked to the edge of the road, placed one of Kathy's Gremlin Bells[7] on the grass underneath the hotel sign, acknowledging that she, too, had completed the ride!

Riding home, I could feel my mind was jumbled. I had been blessed by a well-timed visit from a biker guardian angel, a Rider of the Storm, so to speak, and I learned I had the endurance to ride cross-country on my motorcycle. I had finished the ride, Kathy and I had set out to complete one year before. I had spent several days relaxing on the beach with that, nowhere to go, nowhere to be, feeling yet I felt emotionally drained, and empty as I rolled into my garage!

I arrived home not knowing how to fill the gap of emptiness scrambled up inside. Knowing I was still vulnerable to falling back into that dark world, I knew staying as close to my faith as possible was a given. Being a member of a large Methodist Church made it easy to stay connected with many different ministries, and my involvement needed to stay intentional, which it did. I also returned to work after being off for an extended period due to the accident. However, returning to work would bring about its own elevated stress level.

But the one thing I could not get off my mind from the trip was that Rider of the Storm. Out of nowhere, he arrives on his motorcycle to put on rain gear, at the exact moment I'm pulling over to do the same! He senses my fear of pulling onto the shoulder of the road and creates a radiating calm effect inside me! When I told him about the accident, his empathetic tears were the kind that made me feel he had a personal connection to

---

- [7]Rooted in biker folklore, a tradition, more common among Harley Davidson riders, where a small bell is attached to the lowest section of a motorcycle, believed to ward off evil road spirits or "gremlins" that cause mechanical problems and accidents. A rider cannot buy their own bell; it Must be gifted to the rider.

Kathy and me. Who was he, this Rider of the Storm? Was he my Biker Guardian Angel?

There was a spiritual force surrounding the entire incident!

Another Lesson Learned, Another Grace Moment!

Since driving on my Road to Damascus, I have been blessed with so many grace moments. There will be many more coming in the future, leading me to the Other Side of Life! Time will continue to march on, and as it does, I will learn another valuable lesson!

Some things just can't be explained!

7.
Real Family Love, but No More Answers

"Hope is willing to leave unanswered questions unanswered and unknown futures unknown. Hope makes you see God's guiding hand not only in the gentle and pleasant moments but also in the shadows of disappointment and darkness."

— Henri Nouwen[8]

Yes, what's next, God? That is what I would ask God each day after finishing my morning prayers, but most days came and went without so much as a whisper from Jesus. In retrospect, my mind may not have been too focused on what would come next. It was a jumbled mess, and the stress I was dealing with was also harming my health.

With great encouragement from my children, I chose to semi-retire in 2013 from a lengthy career in accounting. It would be less stressful, and I would have more time to begin some hobbies, write a book or two, and take a few more cross-country motorcycle trips. The ingredients of the Obstacles and the Crucible were, at times, dragging me into the abyss of that dark world. Staying intentional, using all the tools I had in my wheelhouse, especially keeping close to my faith family, were the solutions during that time of need.

After my retirement, I saddled up and took those few more cross-country trips, and Jesus and I had some lengthy discussions while I was on the road. Those road trips taught me many lessons about my faith and gave me a few more grace moments I'll never forget. As I thought about my many grace moments, I remembered just a few I received from Jesus, bringing Kathy into my life.

During my many road trips to Florida, when I visited Kathy's family, I would stay at their homes instead of a hotel, making my stay incredibly special. They and I had become close, and they treated me like

---

[8] Henri Nouwen, Turn My Mourning into Dancing, (Thomas Nelson, Inc., 2004), 60

another family member. Some may wonder why that would be so special. Well, I never knew family love while I was growing up. My home life was filled with so much anger and arguing there was never time for love!

My adult life continued the same as my youth; anger filled it day by day. Then one day, in my early 50s, I drove my Road to Damascus, where I met up with Jesus, who redefined my life. And then I met Kathy, who introduced me to a different kind of family—a family that talks and doesn't scream. A family who made me feel loved, respected, and accepted! And to me, that was incredibly special!

Kathy showed me what true family love felt like; love that wasn't about conflict, but about understanding and acceptance. She helped me see that forgiveness wasn't just for others, it was for myself too. She was quite an independent soul who touched the hearts of so many and will be forever missed! Another teaching moment came about as I thought of the Gospel of Mark and how Jesus preached of the closeness between biological family and those who are like family. *"Whoever does God's will, is my brother and sister and mother."* (Mark 3:35 NIV). To be part of a family doesn't mean you must share the same DNA. It means you truly share a familial type of love for each other, and that is what I found in Kathy's family.

From 2013 through 2015, those cross-country motorcycle trips filled my life with fun and excitement. They also taught me more spiritual lessons and kept me turning the pages of my Bible more often than at any other time in my earlier years.

And then, it happened!

That day finally came for me, when the many questions I had about my birth, why I went to live with my grandparents, would never be answered. It was an event that significantly changed how I extinguished the fires inside the crucible of my past. Friday morning, January 1, I received a phone call from my stepdad telling me my mother had passed the night before, December 31, 2015, due to illness and aging. I at once booked a flight to Chicago, and a few days later, I was settling back into my hometown with my anxiety level running high! On the first day of her wake, I arrived at the funeral parlor earlier than my family, as I needed time to adjust to her death.

As much as we had a relationship most of my life, we were more cordial than close. Whenever we were together, I felt there was something deep inside of her she wished to tell me, but could not find the way to say the words. It seemed to me that something profound inside her heart was causing her discomfort; a soulful, spiritual pain. That day, alone at the funeral parlor, just myself and her deceased body lying still in the casket, I saw, for the first time, in all the years I had known her, a woman who was finally at peace. Christ already greeted her soul into heaven, saying to her My good and faithful servant, you are home. In John's gospel, he writes, *"Jesus says to her, 'I am the resurrection and the life. The one who believes in me will live, even though they die; and whoever lives by believing in me will never die. Do you believe this?'"* (John 11:25-26 NIV). I honestly believe that as she passed from our realm to God's kingdom of heaven, that is how he greeted her.

There were so many things I wish we could have talked about. Although my mother had never received a college degree, she had worked in the accounting profession her entire life and was exceptionally good. I also sought a career in the same profession, receiving my B.S. in Accounting. I had always wished for her to tell me she was proud of me, but I never heard those words! I had prayed to Jesus most of my life for her honesty, as far as whether I was going to be given up for adoption. Was that why my grandparents stepped in to raise me? So many questions and now, no answers, the ones she held the key for unlocking. Questions I had wanted answers to for so long. Again, just like my visit with my pastor, my life seemed filled with questions that would never have answers!

I wished we could have mended so many fences, so many hurts, connected so many of life's dots that I had wanted for so long to be connected, and as all this crossed through my mind, as strange as it was, I felt a sense of peace. It was at that funeral parlor that I was able to see and feel the many valuable lessons my travels through the dark night of the soul were trying to teach me. It was as if Christ was right there telling me, *It is time!* Time to lay down the crucible I had been carrying for too many years. The weights need to drop; the past is the past, so begin living in the moment!

We all met up for a luncheon after my mother's funeral. I then hopped on a plane and flew back to OKC. As the plane wheels left the ground, I looked out the window, blew an imaginary kiss downward, and lay my head back. It had all started with a mom giving birth to a baby boy at Englewood Hospital in Chicago, IL, on a cloudy day in October 1954, and 3 separate decisions made by four adults. The wrestling, the struggle, the heartaches, the complicated feelings of the adults involved, and the little boy who was collateral damage from those decisions. Through the years, it seemed to all fall apart, yet somehow found its way back to a sense of healing for that little boy, now a much older man, on that frigid 5th day of January 2016.

I do believe I was presented with a few grace moments during my stay in Chicago and my presence at my mother's funeral. During those few days, I began finding my true self, unburying myself from the darkness of the road I had been traveling on for a long time. It was saying goodbye to my mother, knowing the questions didn't need to be answered, for me to live to my full potential. I realized I could let go of some parts of the crucible I had been carrying, but I also knew there was more left to conquer.

But through it all, I recognized that Jesus had granted me more grace moments than I could ever begin to count. Many times, in my distant past, I called something that happened "a close call" or "a coincidence." During those times when Jesus and I were distant, he was still close by, watching over me and granting me grace moments. Then the ones I knew about: driving on my road to Damascus, signing up for a dating site, meeting Kathy, and so many more.

I knew there were still a few more issues within the crucible I needed to address before I could finally say goodbye to it. We're getting to those soon!

8.

Jesus, the Road, Music, and The Last Ride

"Every New Beginning Comes
From Some Other Beginnings End."
—Lucius Annaeus Seneca

Plane wheels down, back in OKC with much going on, and before I knew it, it was summertime and the weather was hot! Wow, it had already been six years since the night that catapulted my life into a different existence. So many of my life experiences have taken place since the day my dear friend and pastor challenged me to ask God what was to come next in my life. I knew I needed to find new beginnings, ways to bring me back to a feeling of peace and joy, calmness, and serenity. But how?

I began to receive what I felt were the answers to my questions, as if God had opened the pages of the Book of Proverbs, telling me in a loud voice to read. *"Trust in the Lord with all your heart and lean not on your own understanding."* (Proverbs 3:5 NIV). As I read, I began to put the pieces together. What is it I must do to make way for new beginnings?

I began thinking of how being close to the ocean brought me a feeling of calmness, a sense of peace, and joy. And how being on the road, just me, my bike, my music, and my Jesus, was as pure as it could get. Was it time for another road trip to Florida and the ocean? One more time! It did have a beginning, July 9, 2010, the night my world stood still, and now it's time for an ending! It's time for one Last Ride.

And so, I coined it to be forever known as The Last Ride! The ride began June 17, 2016, and ended on Thursday, July 7, with a long ride home from Opelousas, LA, 580 miles, total trip 21 days, total of 3,956 miles. More historical knowledge learned, fun and laughter had with family, and terrific people met along the journey. Caught a snag during the early afternoon of my 2nd day, which quickly shuttled me back to the evening of July 9, 2010.

An unexpected thunderstorm dropped on top of me while traveling on I-10, between Lafayette and Baton Rouge, over the Atchafalaya Swamp Basin, home to a million or more gators. For the first time in many years, I found myself riding with fear surrounding me. I wasn't afraid of dying because of the weather or traffic conditions. I was fearful of dying by the razor-sharp teeth of over a million gators. The bridge shoulder was quite narrow; the concrete embankments were about 36" tall. If I ran off the road, I would be thrown from my motorcycle, falling into the bayou, and I would be the Lunch Special for the gators!

The rain ended, and I made it into Biloxi, checking into my hotel and ending the day with a cold beer and a great shrimp dinner. But after riding along that bridge, wind gusts howling and rain pelting down on me, I had to ask myself one big question! Why did I continue to make this 4,000-mile road trip every year? What was I searching for? I knew the more I asked myself those questions, the more I would turn around and ask God the same questions. I also knew the answers were not going to come easy. Little did I realize I was still a few years away from getting the answers I needed to hear!

Well, a good night's sleep, and it was time to continue my ride, and away I went. The stops included a quick lunch at the FloraBama Beach Bar in Perdido Key, FL, a few days in St. Augustine, a beautiful, breathtaking ride along A1A, hugging the Atlantic coast, and a few days visiting family. From there, it was a fantastic morning ride across the Overseas Highway, U.S. Highway 1, for 4 days in Key West. Great site seeing, and crazy times for nighttime entertainment along Duval Street. From Key West, it was back on the road for 4th of July celebrations at Clearwater Beach and then the long trip home.

It was a long road trip vacation, 21 days of Zoom, Zoom; almost 4,000 miles traveled, and each day began with my daily prayers and the reading of a devotional. Each morning, I would ask God what was next, and every day I would hope he would answer. And each morning as I hit the road, I would listen to "The Road and the Radio."[9] by Kenny Chesney, my morning mantra.

---

[9] Kenny Chesney, "The Road and the Radio," *The Road and the Radio*, BNA Records, 2005

So, there it is, folks, a capsulized version of my Last Ride. A few questions answered and yet many more left to go!! During this Last Ride, I realized I would not find many of the answers I was looking for while traveling on two wheels down to the southeast section of the country. Motorcycle riding gave me much pleasure over many years. As much as I loved the sun on my face and the wind at my back, riding also proved to be an emotional and psychological goblin that 100 Gremlin Bells could not fight. So, I parked my motorcycle in the garage and again, began another quest into the unknown.

Two years later, in the summer of 2018, I would return to the Gulf coast of Florida, not on two wheels, but on a plane ride and a rented car. That time, not for a simple afternoon siesta on the beach. Nope, that time would be to explore new places to live.

God, What's Next?

9.

Goodbye Zoom, Zoom! Hello, Coastal Sunshine

"When I let go of what I am, I become what I might be.
When I let go of what I have, I receive what I need."[10]
— John Heider

After my Last Ride, I sat back in my wicker chair, still asking God the same questions. But now, I was ready for the answers; or at least, to listen for them more closely. Continuing to pray, I reviewed all I had been through since the day I traveled on my Road to Damascus. I had become a different person that day, filled with positive emotions. It was after that day I met and married Kathy, and we were so truly in love with each other, but I also watched her die. I had moved back to my old house and completed an overhaul of its interior, but the memories of me and her remained. The review took me back to the chaos of my childhood, the way it had followed me into adulthood. Letting go of unanswered questions at my mother's funeral, I felt confident that much of my burden would be lifted. But I discovered there were still lingering issues that just wouldn't let go of me.

This analysis also took me back to my cross-country motorcycle trips and the many miles I rode! Why did I do it? It was after my Last Ride that I realized the answers to the questions I needed were never going to be found out on the road. The excitement, the thrill, was on the road, but the answers to the questions I needed were only going to be found inside my own heart and soul and through my love of Christ.

So, I sat in my backyard praying and listening, listening as I asked "God, What's Next?"

I began to think back to my teenage years and how I got involved with motorcycles. Motorcycles and fast cars were the things for guys back when I was a teenager. I was 17, a hippie, and had long hair and a fast car. My family considered me a rebel, so why not add motorcycle riding to

---

[10] John Heider, *The Tao of Leadership* (Green Dragon Books, 2015), 33

round out my teen years? My fast car was a ‘67 Chevy Malibu, 327 CI, over 370 HP, turning high 12’s in the quarter mile at the drag strip. But I wanted another fast car, so I bought a shell of a ‘57 Chevy Bel Air with a straight axle and towed it home in hopes of building another fast car. Shell meaning no engine and no interior; yuk, yuk! Well, my hopes never materialized, and since I was working as an auto mechanic, I knew another mechanic selling his motorcycle, a 1968 Honda 305. He wanted my ’57 Chevy, so we traded! He got the ’57 Chevy, I got the bike plus $200.00.

It was quite a long journey to get started riding motorcycles. So, I sold my ’67 Malibu. Drag racing was and still is a costly sport! The Honda 305, well, it took me a while to learn how to ride a motorcycle, and a few weeks later, Oops! But I traded up for a Honda 450 and sold the bike just before I got married. She said I could keep the golf clubs, but the bike had to go.

However, not the end of the story! A mechanic friend I rode with had a Harley Sportster, and we envied him. The way he sat in the saddle, the way he gripped his bars, the sound of his pipes, just how I had ever dreamt a motorcycle should be. But it was much more expensive than I could afford at 18. I promised myself that if the chance ever came again for me to be riding two wheels, it would be a Harley-Davidson. Well, it took many years, but that day came in April 2007.

After many years away and getting back on a motorcycle in 2007, it became a part of me, an extension of who I was. People were amazed at how I rode in all kinds of weather, from sun and warmth to rain and cold. But after July 9, 2010, riding just wasn’t the same. I would always be looking on my right-hand side, wanting, hoping to see her glowing smile! But it wasn’t there! I tried for many years to glaze over, to camouflage how riding had lost its glow, its magic, since she had passed, but again it was something I could not run from anymore. It was time to say Goodbye; Goodbye to the Zoom, Zoom of Riding!

And so, it began! On July 2, 2019, I sold my 2011 Harley-Davidson Street Glide. I had covered many miles with that bike, in all kinds of weather conditions, but I knew that for me to make the changes I needed to make, major paradigm shifts in my life needed to happen. But I was still in my same backyard, wondering why I was having a tough time connecting the way I felt I should be with Christ.

And the more I prayed, the more images of the beach continued to be planted in my brain. Somehow, not knowing how it happened, I thought back to a business conference I had attended many years before in Miami, Florida. I remember telling myself when I was there that someday I would live near the beach. The thought continued to be in the far reaches of my mind like an anchor for all those years. I wondered if that was what God had been nudging me with. Was that the way of making new beginnings, too? Was that the answer I had been looking for, for me to find hope, a new future, and finally peace and joy?

I was free to move, as my part-time client gig was remote and I could work anywhere I would plant myself. But I worried about how my children would handle my move to Florida. Much to my surprise, they all agreed, all wanting happiness for my life. So, 2 years after my Last Ride, I would find myself back along the Southwest Coast of Florida scoping out places to live in Fort Myers, FL. All indicators pointed me toward the move, yet I continued to wonder whether I was running to something or from something. In retrospect, I can now see how Jesus was mysteriously uncovering the path before me, leading me to many of the answers I looked for.

Many say the things that keep you from moving forward or fear the most are the things you trust God the least with. This seemed true for me, but it was confusing and paradoxical, as I realized the venture into the unknown was frightening me. But I also knew every time I threw my leg over my motorcycle, I was venturing into the unknown, and I knew God was watching over me. Why was a move to Florida any different?

As I was mustering the courage to follow God's wishes, my oldest son from my first marriage, now living in Florida, asked if I would agree for him and me to live together after I moved to Florida. He was highly educated but had fallen victim to a severe psychological illness many years before, could no longer work, and was on disability. I knew saying yes may be disastrous. I eventually agreed, continuing to believe God was speaking to me in mysterious ways.

So, somehow, through divine intervention, my house sold within one day, and I quickly flew down to Fort Myers and rented a condo three miles from the beach. Setting out with a new course for life just a few days before the change of seasons, my hopes were that I heard the answers to my prayers correctly and that Jesus was guiding my way!

Wild as the wind and calm as the sea, my life's direction changed again toward the Southwest coast of Florida. On Tuesday morning, September 3, 2019, I embarked upon a daring adventure in the planning stages for over two years. The crazy and much speculative idea, hatched from a highly wild, wacky, and youthful dream 35 years before, was happening, so I could create a new life path. I was departing from the city I had called home for 18 years, leaving behind my kids and grandkids, my tremendous family and loyal friends, my faithful church family who had stood by my side through laughter and grief, all in hopes of finding the answers to the many questions that I felt still needed answering.

My emotions were standing on end with a euphoric jubilance, anticipating the incredible voyage I was undertaking. I was confident Jesus had blessed me with the level of wisdom needed for such a challenging and life-changing decision. And so, a bright new future was born, and off I went to the Sunshine State, where alligators hold kings court in the freshwater ponds and youthful kids listen intently to the many stories of pirate folklore southwest Florida has to offer.

Was moving to the City of Palms the right decision to make? I knew it wasn't a sure thing, but I believed it was where God had directed me to be. As much as I was leaving behind so many memories, I was simultaneously carrying an overwhelming weight of tragedy and grief along with the many childhood pains I had not been able to let go of with my mother's death. The ones that would unsuspectingly engulf and entrap me and draw me back into that murky world, keeping me from moving forward with many new chapters of my life I so lovingly deserve!

The agreement with my son was a 2-year plan. After 2 years, I would be solo long-term. But as the story played out over the second week, the future became darker. Unplanned events began taking place. The once-miracle dream took on an ugly face, followed by an experience I had hoped and prayed would not happen! My son changed his mind and chose not to stay with me. I knew with his psychological illness, the possibility was there for him to change his mind. I also knew changing his mind would possibly burden our relationship, which did, unfortunately, happen.

By then, I was relying heavily on Apostle Paul's words for guidance. I picked up my Bible and read from his letter to the church of Philippi. *"Do not be anxious about anything, but in every situation, by prayer and petition, with thanksgiving, present your requests to God. And the peace of God, which transcends all understanding, will guard your hearts and minds in Christ Jesus."* (Philippians 4:6-7 NIV). Well, through my interpretation of God's direction for my future, I was there, and that is where I'll be! At least for now!

I knew Jesus had pointed me to this place for a reason. Was it to be long-term or temporary? Was it to help me find the answers I had been searching for? Only time would tell. I knew it would be a money stressor as my son was to be sharing expenses, but I'll get by! And I was planning on being here alone anyway! And now I'm here, it's time to enjoy life, discover unexplored places, and follow Jesus' lead while I search for my answers. Something inside told me that if I continue in that direction, I'll pull back the onion peels to find many of those answers I had been waiting to see.

I again found myself at another life-changing crossroads, with the future unknown. But as much as I was shocked, I surprised myself with a tremendous lack of fear, knowing the future is in the hands of Jesus and there is no way for me to know my future, so why worry about it? As I assimilated into my new surroundings and a much different life plan, my mind and soul developed more clarity of life than I had felt in many years. I created an attitude of discernment that I would be experiencing, which would become a more profound spiritual undertaking that would, again, change my life.

10.
My Year of the Pirate

"...Life is about not knowing, having to change, taking the moment, and making the best of it, without knowing what's going to happen next..."[11]
-- **Gilda Radner**

Originally planned to be my forever home in retirement, it turned into what could only be described as an extremely chaotic 1 year, which would include the wildest time our world had seen in almost 100 years. For me, this would be My Year of the Pirate! It was the year I became a metaphorical adventurous, opportunistic pirate of sorts, boarding my own mythical pirate ship, casting off the anchors of past crucibles that had kept me weighted down for too long. This new existence as a mythical pirate, still undefined, might provide me with a creative atmosphere of reinvention into a nowhere to go, nowhere to be lifestyle. It is now time for me to relax, enjoy the beach, the ocean, allowing the miracles of God to soak into my heart and soul, and to let the sun and the surf do its rejuvenation. I was running on empty, and my heart and soul were in desperate need of redemption. Sitting in the sand, gazing out, watching the sun set into the horizon always made me feel so close to Jesus. That was where I needed to be at that time in my life!

As I awoke to the sun shining bright in the eastern sky, a mere 6 weeks from leaving the Sooner state, I began that special day with my morning coffee, daily devotional and a Bible Scripture for the day from the Book of Proverbs, *"In their hearts humans plan their course, but the Lord establishes their steps."* (Proverbs 16:9 NIV). The day was Wednesday, October 9, 2019, which would have been mine and Kathy's 10th Wedding Anniversary. There were still many more questions that I needed to have answered as I was moving forward. I knew I was free of so many hurts and pains after saying goodbye to my mother as she lay in her casket, but still, many left. I knew if I didn't find a way to bring them to the surface, say goodbye, and drop them deep into the proverbial depths of the ocean, every October 9th, the dark night of the soul would find me.

---

[11] Gilda Radner, *It's Always Something,* (New York: Simon & Schuster, 2015), 254

As much as I could have allowed that day to become a villain, lighting a fuse with melancholy fears, I chose to allow my daily devotional words and Scripture to be an inspiration and spend the day at the beach. The majestic and powerful ocean view reminded me of how small I was next to the vastness of the sea and the world around me. The more I stared out at the beautiful horizon that morning, I thought of how wide and long, and high, and deep, God's love is for me. And I began to remember some of Kathy's and my most magical moments when we had our arms wrapped tightly around each other in deep prayer, while in Worship service, praising our Lord and Savior.

As I stood on the beach, casting my sight as far as I could see, in awe of the beauty of one of God's miracles to man, a leaping dolphin came popping out of the surface of the ocean. I knew, without delay, I needed to find those answers that would point me in a much different direction for my life and my future. I didn't seem to be finding the answers as quickly as I had hoped for, and again, I was feeling uneasy about my move. It was through the direction of God that I moved to Florida, so why was I still feeling distraught about being there? I went back to OKC for both Thanksgiving and Christmas, returning to Fort Myers after Christmas. I was missing my kids and grandkids, but I didn't feel I misread God's message to me. Arriving back to my new home at the condo, I was truly torn. There I was again, screaming out to Jesus, *"Why am I here? Did I hear you wrong and misread everything I thought you were telling me? Is this where I'm supposed to be, or was this just another one of those things I thought I heard you say to me?"*

I could not shake the churning in my stomach. I began to think more seriously about a conversation I had with the senior pastor of the Methodist Church I had been attending in Fort Myers. During our meeting, after giving him a brief description of my background and how I arrived in Fort Myers, he said to me, paraphrased, "There will always be doubt about whether you made the right decision about moving here, until you choose to get off the fence. On the day you choose to transfer your membership from your Methodist Church in OKC to this church in Fort Myers, it will be the day you say, I'm here in Fort Myers permanently. But until that day comes, you'll stay on the fence." Thinking back to that conversation shook me.

The next morning, I ventured over the Causeway to Sanibel beach, and the Sanibel lighthouse for much needed spiritual guidance that day. Did I blow it? Was this just a silly kid's dream I was playing out in my mind that became reality? I was again estranged from my son, and I moved almost 1,600 miles away from the rest of my kids and my grandkids. I sold my house and furniture, packed what little I had left, and drove here, for what? I thought I heard the message from Jesus clearly and loudly. But now, I'm not so sure!

As I sat in the sand directly under the Sanibel lighthouse, standing tall and majestic, I prayed to God, asking Him to please tell me, again, why I was there! Somehow, through my tears, listening so very closely, I began to hear God speaking to me. Well, I am quite sure God has dealt with many hardheaded guys like me. So, as I dried my tears and remembered the words of Jeremiah 29:11, it all started to become much clearer. Maybe this move was never meant to be permanent, but a place for learning and short-term refitting, a renewal of my soul.

As all of this became clearer in my mind, I could feel a spiritual presence begin to surround me, and a happy smile came to my face! I stood up, brushed off the sand, and said, *"Okay, God, show me the lessons I'm to learn."* As I left the beach area, I remembered a great diner that had been on the island for many years, the Sanibel Lighthouse Café. Feeling refreshed, knowing I didn't have to have all the answers yet, I chose to have lunch at the Café. After lunch, back over the Causeway I went, in preparation for a short-term living experience in Fort Myers and the unknown when I return to OKC.

The next few months were spent enjoying the tropics until the world shut down due to the COVID-19 Pandemic. My 1-year short-term move, and learning experience could only be described as extremely chaotic and the craziest Year of the Pirate I will never forget. The time was spent in a mode of meditation and prayer, continuing my daily walks in the park and at the beach. I also continued to contemplate the lessons I was learning just as I felt Jesus had instructed me to do. Walking each day, taking in the beauty of the thick tropical plants, sheltered by a canopy of dense jungle-like forestry, and the immense population of palm trees, gave a landscape ripe for swallowing the many forthcoming lessons.

So, God, What's Next?

11.
Surrender, Forgive, Let It Go

"Surrender is a journey from outer turmoil to inner peace."[12]
--Sri Chinmoy

But then, COVID-19 made Florida surrender, for a brief period. I, too, surrendered my daily walks in the luscious tropical gardens to daily exercising along the streets and highways near my condo. No longer was I seeing the beauty of the tropical flowers and luscious greenery, but now casting my eyes on the ugliness of stagnant water lying in a drainage ditch running along the highway. As my eyes gazed at that repulsive sight each day, I knew Jesus had not brought me this far without making sure every moment became a teaching lesson for me. The stillness of the moss-covered water reminded me I had more burdens to lift from my shoulders. It's time to stop running! Surrender, Forgive, Let It Go!

As for my biological father, who passed away several years ago, and his abandonment of me, the desertion of his fatherly duties, well, he lost out on knowing and loving a great son. In retrospect, it's possible his own cowardice took him to his own dark night of the soul. Through my own experiences, I know how difficult it is to survive the grips of the dark side. I'm sure he's been forgiven by Christ and is somewhere in the Kingdom of heaven. Surrender, Forgive, Let It Go!

As for the teachers, priests, nuns who's job it was to teach me how to reach for the stars and not belittle me or hold me accountable, at such a young age, for the behaviors of others, I know now how easy it can be to be overtaken by a dogma that forces you to feel you are doing God's work when you may be hurting others. Surrender, Forgive, Let It Go!

As for my grandparents, who, to the best of my knowledge, kept me from living through the foster care system, I know they did the best they could, given the emotional tools they had at that time. For as much as my living environment was not conducive to love and affection, they did

---

[12] Sri Chinmoy, *Seventy-Seven Thousand Service Trees,* part 17 (Agni Press 2000) 16587

provide me the best upbringing they knew how. Surrender, Forgive, Let It Go!

As for the many others from my past who may have been a party to the events throughout my childhood and youth, Surrender, Forgive, Let It Go!

I also had to remember those whom I had loved or who had held a level of major importance in my life, that I, too, had caused those same hurts and pains with my words and actions. For all those iniquities, I not only had to own it, but I also had to say, in all sincerity, I am Sorry! I Surrender to you! Forgive Me! Please Let It Go!

I'm certainly not saying it all happened overnight. It was an ongoing process taking place over several years. But it was during that time, my *Year of the Pirate*, many revelations came to me. Revelations about me, what I had gone through, who I was, and who I wanted to become. How do I put peace and joy back into my life in a way that I never lose it, ever again? As I began to feel the impact of the pandemic more, all I could hear were the sound of silence! Time to listen to Jesus speak, and speak He did!

Well, the day finally came, and as I blew a kiss toward the beach, I would say "so long" to Fort Myers. Ironically, although the trailer was packed a little bit heavier than when I moved there, the invisible weights I had been carrying in my "proverbial backpack" for many years felt so much lighter than they had ever felt. I chose that time, during a global pandemic shutdown, to stop and to listen to God's instructions, and to take those sounds of silence to know and realize that I am better than what my past said I was. For that one year, I lived in Fort Myers, my *Year of the Pirate*, by stopping and spending precious time by myself, alone in a faraway and strange land, just me and God, I listened to what God was telling me!

As I look back on that year, I think of a scripture verse found in Proverbs which says, *"Listen, my son, accept what I say, and the years of your life will be many. I instruct you in the way of wisdom and lead you along straight paths."* (Proverbs 4:10 NIV). I opened my ears to hear what God was telling me. He was telling me it's time to set sail back home to OKC. Setting my new course toward OKC, knowing through the divine powers of God's grace and presence, I had found the way to drop most of the weight I had been carrying to the bottom of the ocean. With a much lighter feeling in my emotional being and a new mindset, I knew the answer to finding permanent, forever joy would only be found back home, back to more of the unknown. But this time I'm ready for whatever unfolds.

12.
Chrysalis Moments of Life

"We delight in the beauty of the butterfly,
but rarely admit the changes it has gone through to achieve that beauty."[13]
— Maya Angelou

I arrived back in Oklahoma City during COVID, and at the time my church was streaming Worship services on-line. As the pandemic period ended, people began feeling safer and more comfortable coming back to church in person. Discussions began in late summer of 2022 about starting a Sunday Bible class after our Contemporary Worship service. Suddenly, I was offering to lead the class with my words coming from, *"Who knows where,"* as if there were spiritual voices speaking for me! All I can say is, Jesus knows best!

Knowing the Education Director for many years, she trusted my choices of curriculum for the class. The first session would be a great class about Forgiveness. Leading the class on my first day, I learned quite quickly a study guide only goes so far! The leader must do a great deal of their own homework to be a good leader. Since I aspired to be just that, I dug deeper into the subject, learning all I could. I knew that would help me develop the emotional and spiritual pieces needed to let the final cog of my crucible go in learning how to forgive myself!

Finishing my first class, I had a feeling of joy knowing I had brought myself and my class closer to Jesus Christ. I felt the kind of joy I had been searching for and began to wonder if this could be a way to bring peace and joy back into my life!

As each week's class finished, in my mind, another curtain opened, presenting me more until the entire part of all those past years came into view again. I was back in the mountains, driving my Sebring, knowing I was trying so hard to clear the weeds that had covered my faith in Jesus Christ. Driving on that Interstate roadway, over 6,000 feet in the air,

---

[13] Angelou, Maya. "We delight in the beauty of the butterfly but rarely admit the changes it has gone through to achieve that beauty." *Inspiring Quotes Daily*. May 15, 2023. https://www.inspiringquotesdaily.com/maya-angelou-butterfly-quote/.

feeling it was time to end it all, and then I heard that special song playing on the CD player!

It was on that day, as I cried out to Jesus for help, he responded with such a mighty presence only the he can give. And with that presence, I was lifted and placed back down on my own Road to Damascus. On that day, placed at a Crossroads, given a Choice, I chose to follow Christ. My soul was given a new life, my spirit was restored, and I was sent on a new course of life that day. A course that would present to me some of the worst of times, yet some of the best of times, my life could ever imagine. And through it all, my eyes would be forever directed toward the Cross and Christ.

It was that Chrysalis moment that flashed me back to that incredible day at the pizza parlor, where I met my Anam Cara. That blue-eyed Irish country girl who would become my loving wife, married on October 9, 2009, by our dear friend and faithful pastor. And, sadly, that Chrysalis moment would take me back to the evening of July 9, 2010, when both of us would temporarily die, but I would soon be told; *Sorry, it is not your time,* but Kathy, my bride, would travel on her winged Harley Davidson motorcycle to heaven, leaving me behind.

It was at that Chrysalis moment I remembered the young boy who would hold my lifeless hand at the accident scene and speak the words to me: "Come back, come back to us." That moment when I would leave the accident scene, be taken to the hospital, and only then would I learn of my Anam Cara's passing from our daughter. The same Chrysalis moment that would place me several weeks later, sobbing on the shoulder of my pastor, asking the question, "Why am I still here, and she died?" That same moment, I would think of the hug he gave me and faithfully explain to me, to continue following a healing path, you must now ask God; *What's next for my life?*

A Chrysalis moment that forced me to look back at the many roads I had traveled for all those years, some being straight as an arrow, yet some filled with winding curves. Many days the sun would shine brightly in the sky, yet there were those where the thunder and lightning crackled and lit up the sky as only a perfect storm of life could bring. A Chrysalis moment where I remembered the many days and nights, I would hear Coulda, Shoulda, Woulda, and I would plunge into the dark night of the soul, but I knew my spirit shadow would always be there walking with me, holding my hand as I meandered my way back from that temporary visit to the dark side.

A Chrysalis moment that reminded me of that sunny day in September 2019, when I ventured out toward Southwest Florida, in what became My Year of the Pirate. That moment also reminded me, as much as that year created hardships between my son and I, it also became a year of many grace moments gifted to me by my Lord and Savior, Jesus Christ. It was during that Year of the Pirate, I learned about the many gifts that can be granted to a person when they sit alone in the sounds of silence, after praying, and listening to the answers God has in store for them.

It was during that time, I sat silently one beautiful evening, listening to the sounds of silence as the sun set below the western horizon, asking the question again, "Is this it? What if living my life, the best I can, by the Golden Rule, becoming closer to my faith in Christ, is my true purpose? Could that be the way I bring true peace and joy back into my life?

My travels as a metaphorical pirate, my ups and downs traveling through the dark night of the soul, surviving, and letting go of all my emotional baggage still left over, and finally listening to God, while spending time in the sounds of silence, brought a level of peace to my life, more than I have known in a very long time. I had found such great happiness, fun, laughter, acceptance, love, joy, and peace through my profound love for Kathy, and then she died, and all of that disappeared.

Through the course of those many years, I learned, in many ways, how to put all of that back into my life except peace and joy. My joy and peace seemed to be gone forever! I had been starved of peace and joy since Kathy had been killed. Maybe it was not just the want and need of permanent joy I was looking for; maybe I was searching for redemption.

As I pondered on that one item and if that was the single reason I was allowing joy to elude me, I thought to the words the apostle Paul wrote to the church of Corinth, saying; *"It is because of him that you are in Christ Jesus, who has become for us wisdom from God, that is our righteousness, holiness and redemption."* (1 Corinthians 1:30 NIV). And then I remembered the most important thing more than anything else, Jesus died on the cross and was resurrected for me, for us, to give us salvation and redemption from all our sins. I figured that was good enough for me to begin letting joy back into my life.

That Chrysalis moment also taught me; it is not bad to find joy in another human being, especially one that you love as dearly as I loved Kathy. But when it comes to forever peace and forever joy, linked with a taste of serenity and tranquility, and expecting all from another human is, well, very unnatural. That human you love so dearly will eventually split from you or die. I believe it's okay to hang on to all those beautiful attributes that your loved ones give you, but, my recommendation is to never ever lose sight of the fact only through God will we find true and forever peace and joy. No matter how deep your love is for that other human or their love for you, we humans separate, whether by splitting the relationship or death, and with that comes the death of joy, and we will be disappointed. The good news is if we choose to place our joy in Christ and find our peace in Christ, and we know Christ never leaves us, we will forever be filled with peace and joy, and we will never be disappointed. Why, because our Lord and Savior never disappoints, and He loves us unconditionally.

It was at that Chrysalis moment I realized, That's It! Allowing my peace in life to come from Christ and choosing to find my joy in Christ, Was It! I think again about the apostle Paul and his words to the Galatians, when he wrote, *"But the fruit of the Spirit is love, joy, peace, forbearance, kindness, goodness, faithfulness, gentleness, and self-control. Against such things there is no law."* (Galatians 5:22-23 NIV). Choosing to allow joy back into my heart through my love for Christ, and knowing Christ will never leave me, gives me forever joy in my heart. Could it really be that easy? No, folks, it wasn't as easy as my writings have proved. It's been a long, arduous journey across many rough seas to arrive at the point I'm at in life.

I've been sincerely blessed to have had a support network as I've had but most importantly, I've had Christ holding my hand the entire journey. And He's not just held my hand; He has taken me on a teaching journey that has brought me full circle. I certainly do not remember the day, but I do know, it was at St. Irenaeus Catholic Church in Park Forest, IL, with me being less than 1 year old, when Father Coogan doused my forehead with holy water and said the words similar to; I baptize you in the name of the Father, the Son, and the Holy Spirit, Amen. I feel I have come full circle, being baptized again.

As I look back on my many voyages, each one a lesson being taught in its own distinct way, bringing me to my many Chrysalis moments, I reflect on a few more thoughts. As I say my morning prayers each day, I ask my Holy Spirit to help me to be a kinder, gentler, calmer, and more loving person than I was the day before. I have concluded that as long as I'm improving my life according to *The Golden Rule,* then I'm doing a good thing. Also, since I have been a Methodist for almost 20 years of my life, I strive each day to live by the Three Simple Rules of a Wesleyan Way of Living, to Do No Harm, to Do Good, and Stay in Love with God.[14]

I write these words for all that they may shine a light over you, place a smile on your face, or reacquaint you with and bring you closer to Christ. Not a day goes by I stop thinking of that day I opened my grandma's Bible to the page where I found the words of the prophet Jeremiah 29:11. And I'm reminded every day, with the medal I wear around my neck, the power of the words the apostle Paul wrote in his letter to the church of Philippi, reminding them as much as he could be reminding us with that same letter today; *"I can do all things through Christ who strengthens me."* (Philippians 4:13 NKJV).

It was a Chrysalis moment. I thought of all the crazy metaphorical oceans I've traveled, the twists and turns, ups and downs, laughter, fun, sadness, and grief I've been through for so many years, and as I do, I think of two things. First, I think about The Wizard of Oz and how "Glinda, the Good Witch, revealed to Dorothy that she had always possessed the power to return home."[15] She had to have that yearning, that uncontrollable desire, that hunger, that thirst, to know how to return home. I had to learn for myself, during my most desperate times of life; those times that emotionally drove me to have a yearning, an uncontrollable desire, a hunger, a thirst to know the true meaning of the words of Corrie ten Boom

---

[14] Job, Rueben P, *Three Simple Rules, A Wesleyan Way of Living*, (Nashville, Abingdon Press 2007) 19, 33, 51
[15] L. Frank Baum, *The Wonderful Wizard of Oz* (Chicago: George M. Hill Co., 1900) 256

when she said, "You can never learn that Christ is all you need, until Christ is all you have."[16]

Second, I think of a song by Tim McGraw, Standing Room Only[17] and I think of a day in March 2023, when I attended the memorial service for my cousin's daughter, who had been killed in a mid-air collision while piloting and teaching a student in a small aircraft in Central FL. At the youthful age of 23, this young lady, although not perfect in any way, seemed to hand out a glow of perfection to everyone she met. Every time I would visit with her, sit and talk with her, she glowed with the faithfulness many her age dream of having. As I looked around the church during her service, it was hard to see the walls, as it was truly SRO. As I traveled to the cemetery, I looked out the front windshield, and all I could see was a sea of taillights. Looking into my rearview mirror, all I could see was a sea of headlights. It was not only in death, but it was especially in her young and short life, she exuded the teachings of Jesus by loving God with all her heart, soul, and mind, and loving her neighbor as herself. And she did not get to be a lover of Jesus just by being born. She had two parents who were exemplary role models who kept her life directed in the pathways toward Jesus. She'll remain nameless but if and when you experience those tough times in life when maybe, you feel distant from your faith, think of her or pick up this book and I am sure you will find the inspiration you'll need to say to Jesus, drive my car, steer my boat or fly my plane, 'cause I can't do it alone anymore.

It was in that Chrysalis moment, I discovered I had a feeling of happiness and pleasure caused by something exceptionally good, which is my faith in Christ. I was also feeling I had a certain state of mind brought about by serenity, tranquility through the absence of anxiety and worry related to my faith in Christ. It was in that Chrysalis moment I discovered I had finally found everlasting peace and joy through Jesus Christ. I also knew then that my sense of living in paradise is found in my heart and in my love for Jesus. This has been the story of My Journey, and how I found my way back to a life of Peace and Joy in Christ and through Christ! It has

---

[16] "You can never learn that Christ is all you need, until Christ is all you have" — Corrie ten Boom

[17] McGraw, Tim. "Standing Room Only." Standing Room Only, Big Machine Records, 2023.

Comes from a traditional Gaelic blessing often attributed to St. Patrick been a long, long journey; years upon years, decades upon decades, but I have arrived! But I didn't get here alone. I've arrived due to the many who have loved me and supported me for so many years, when I felt the going was too tough.

Yes, I have arrived at the Other Side of Life, and my hopes and prayers are you have found inspiration in my writings to know that no matter how down you get, no matter how hard life gets, you are not alone. I have found that no matter which road I took, my Lord and Savior was and is there to hold my hand through the best of times and the worst of times. It was the apostle Paul who reminds us in his letter to the Romans, *"For I am convinced that neither death nor life, neither angels nor demons, neither the present nor the future, nor any powers, neither height nor depth, nor anything else in all creation, will be able to separate us from the love of God that is in Christ Jesus our Lord."* (Romans 8:38-39 NIV). I will never allow anyone or anything to ever again separate me from God, and I pray the same for you.

So, there you have it! I have journeyed my own Road to Damascus, took A Leap of Faith, and in doing so, heard a voice, felt a fresh wind, and found Redemption and Salvation through the Cross & Jesus Christ!

And now, as I'm enjoying each day, I must ask,

God, What's Next?

Acknowledgements

I wish to thank my family, friends and my St. Luke's Methodist Church faith family, especially the clergy and staff, for the loving support, emotionally and spiritually, you have all given me. I thank Jesus Christ daily for having each of you in my life!

www.faithjourney54.com

BIBLIOGRAPHY

Angelou, Maya. "We delight in the beauty of the butterfly but rarely admit the changes it has gone through to achieve that beauty." *Inspiring Quotes Daily*. May 15, 2023. https://www.inspiringquotesdaily.com/maya-angelou-butterfly-quote/.

Aurelius, Marcus. Meditations. Translated by George Long, Book 4, Section 3, Dover Publications, 1997.

Baum, L. Frank. *The Wonderful Wizard of Oz*. Chicago: George M. Hill Company, 1900.

Bon Jovi. "Livin on a Prayer." Slippery When Wet, Mercury Records, 1986

Carrie Underwood. "Jesus Take the Wheel." Some Hearts, Arista Nashville, November 15, 2005, Track # 4, Compact Disc

Corrie ten Boom— "You can never learn that Christ is all you need, until Christ is all you have"

Kenny Chesney, "The Road and the Radio," *The Road and the Radio*, BNA Records, 2005

McGraw, Tim. "Standing Room Only." Standing Room Only, Big Machine Records, 2023.

Near Death Experience Research Foundation, Rolling Meadows, IL. Dr. Jeffrey Long, MD. Nderf.org, Don B NDE 16050 Submission date 11/4/2010

Gilda Radner, *It's Always Something,* (New York: Simon & Schuster, 2015), 254

Henri Nouwen, Turn My Mourning into Dancing, (Thomas Nelson, Inc., 2004), 60

Job, Rueben P., *Three Simple Rules, A Wesleyan Way of Living*, (Nashville, Abingdon Press, 2007) 19, 33, 51

John Heider, *The Tao of Leadership* (Green Dragon Books, 2015), 33

Schwartz, Morrie. Tuesdays with Morrie. Kindle, Page 121

Sri Chinmoy, *Seventy-Seven Thousand Service Trees,* part 17 (Agni Press 2000) 16587

Prayers, Quotes & Other:

- Gremlin Bells: Rooted in biker folklore, a tradition, more common among Harley Davidson riders, where a small bell is attached to the lowest section of a motorcycle, believed to ward off evil road spirits or "gremlins" that cause mechanical problems and accidents. A rider cannot buy their own bell; it Must be gifted to the rider.
- Irishcentral.com: St. Patrick's Breastplate: the prayer of Ireland's patron saint.

- Traditional Gaelic blessing often attributed to St. Patrick: **"And in all your comings and goings, may you ever have a kindly greeting from them you meet along the road."**

Made in the USA
Coppell, TX
13 March 2026

73809762R00038